Sing Through It

Depression, burnout
and climbing back up

John Slater

ISBN 978-1-7398368-0-1

In writing this book I would like to pour out thanks and love to my wife, my children and family and dear friends. My thanks and eternal gratitude go out to past colleagues and bosses.

My gratitude and thanks also to the following wonderful people who helped me create this book, coached and advised me and made many changes and corrections to my often-poor grammar, punctuation and flow: my Mother, Peter, my brother now of PJS Brightlight Ltd; Brett Read of Safety Leaders Inc; Bruce Basaraba, Russ Scott and Kurt Bose, thank you guys.

Over the last years mental health has climbed the ladder of importance in society recognising the large numbers of people of all ages who suffer from depression and anxiety, and that people maybe can't talk to those around them or have nobody to talk to. Recognising the symptoms of depression and sever anxiety and talking about these symptoms is so important to start and on the road to recovery.

It would impossible to list all the many wonderful helplines staffed by dedicated and trained professionals that are available. If you find yourself with the symptoms of mental illness, some of which are explained in this book, and especially if you feel you have nothing to live for – CALL FOR HELP, search on the web for suicide help lines, please talk to somebody who can help you.

John Slater has worked 36 years in the energy industry, living in seven countries across five continents and visiting dozens more for work. He has filled senior manager and director roles in large and medium sized companies from contractors to energy industry operators. John is at his best leading teams and coaching companies in a world of change and uncertainty. He has consistently delivered sustainable performance improvements in the companies he has worked for with a backdrop of mental health issues he has struggled to acknowledge and talk about. He followed his family into the City of London after University, but remained determined to follow his chosen career path and left the UK at the age of 22 starting his career in the Netherlands with a multinational contracting firm. His marriage at the age of 26 to his wife from South America, the learning of the Spanish language, the acceptance of different cultures and his ability to lead and coach allowed him opportunities across the globe in public and private companies, where he has worked to leave a cultural legacy where people and the planet matter. John has solid and fixed core values that have played a crucial role in his successes as well as being the cause of deep lows in his life, when he admits he fought losing battles and didn't walk away soon enough.

What you're going to read about

1

An introduction to this story

2

The importance of leaders and you

3

A simplistic view of our brains

CHAPTER ONE

An introduction to this story

I'm not a victim, don't seek sympathy and recognise there are so many people in this world, who could tell their stories and you would learn so much more from them.

I'm not a practiced author and have written this book as it came to me. The book has evolved over six months and gone through multiple versions. So please forgive the language, punctuation and more rookie mistakes.

In my mid-fifties I'm more positive and relaxed than I've been for many years. I'm closer to family and friends, happier and confident in work and feel more integral to the world around me. Around me is and isn't 1m, 1km, 100km's nor 1000km's, it's this amazing, complex, populated and precious planet we have been gifted and have an accountability to care for.

I'm starting to sing again, smiling more and working towards a belly laugh. I enjoy my work; am confident in the impact I can have and know that if I arrive at a time when I'm not valued that's a sign I need to move on.

Why I'm telling my story

I am so thankful that I can tell this story, thanks to the ability to receive treatment and see doctors who could help me. I know that not everybody in this world has this facility.

I thought long and hard on putting my story into the public domain and how to best achieve this, as publicising the work puts my past in the open, my experiences, positive and negative, my struggles and to some extent my family's lives. I want to tell my story, talk about my personal experience to help you and others understand that mental illness is all around us and that acknowledging it and talking about it is

> 'From this early age, I enjoyed, indeed escaped the world through singing'

power. We can recognise it in ourselves and others and have the courage to get help or help.

I would like line supervisors, managers and more senior persons to understand the immense impact both positive and negative they can have on the people who work for them, not only on their careers but on their mental health. I would encourage companies to bring emotional intelligence and other leadership skills to the fore and for leaders to be aware of the mental well-being of their people alongside physical well-being and performance.

We should all understand that all our acts, every day, have an impact on something and someone and maybe us (ourselves) and to encourage you to sit back as often as possible to understand your impact on you and others.

I worried about the impact this book would have on my present and future career, then looked back on past roles where I've been effective, driven positive change from a senior level and taken tough decisions with the backdrop of mental illness.

I compared the old me to the evolving me. Today, I'm more focussed, take clearer, quicker and still the occasional tough decision. I manage stress far better than I ever have done in the past, have greater empathy, listen more, let go of opinions and beliefs more readily and am much clearer on my values. Based on this, let's get going.

To Muslim readers of this book, I understand that alcohol is haram, and apologise for the many references to alcohol, however without these references the story wouldn't be complete.

What is this story

This is not advice for how you should live your life, I'm not a professional life coach. Nor is it a detailed commentary on my life nor a CV. It is not meant to be a long list of the mistakes I've made in my life although, as you will read, I have made a number.

It may be a cautionary tale for current or future people who travel and move regularly for work, and those who aspire to further their careers. My hope is that everybody who reads the book takes away something they might change or how they may help others.

For younger people, if you are kind enough to read this book, please focus on health, happiness, family and friends alongside your career. Balance the future with today and today is for enjoying and living.

Regret not listening to good advice."

I have been fortunate to be brought up in a loving house where my father worked hard to ensure we had a good life, indeed he worked very hard, and my mother was dedicated to our upbringing.

I have taken many life decisions mostly with my wife which were good decisions to us at the time, and I don't regret the rich experience my family and me have had moving regularly with my jobs.

My family and me have been so very fortunate to meet wonderful people on our travels and to have seen first-hand some of the poorest communities on the planet and to have helped in our own small ways, but know we could have done more.

> '**My family and I have been very fortunate to meet wonderful people on our travels**'

I do, however, regret not listening to good advice and not reaching out for help and talking about the symptoms of anxiety and depression much earlier in my life. Had I listened and been wiser, I would live all the experiences again and enjoy them so much more and make them richer and more fun and rewarding for my family and others.

There will those who read this book who don't agree with elements or indeed the entire book, and I'm fine with that and thank you for considering the book in the first place.

CHAPTER TWO

The importance of leaders and you

I have not mentioned names from companies I have worked for and have tried to hide people's and company's identities as much as possible, as I hold no grudges and no animosity and am thankful for the experience I have gained and learnings I taken from all situations. However, to eliminate people from this book would be crazy as we spend so much of our time in work in a week and our lives that the people you work with can have a profound impact on the joy of work and life or just as profoundly the opposite.

I have had the privilege of working with bosses, colleagues, consultants and contractors, people I still look up to, respect and remember fondly and in many cases, who have become friends. A boss who exhibits emotional intelligence seeks to understand their people, motivates, listens and values those who they work

'I've come to learn over the years that we are all driven to do what we do by many factors, and looking back on leaders I've been at odds with, I should have focussed much more on the "why" they said and did what they did. In some cases, this may have helped lower conflict and stress, and in others, looking back, it would not have helped at all.'

with and who work for them. The same goes for companies who listen to their people and value ideas and feedback.

Companies that have and will continue to thrive, increasingly, need to demonstrate their care for staff as well as those they impact as well as demonstrating action to protect the environment, both locally and globally, amongst other attributes. The leaders, from the Board and Executive Management downwards set the standard for behaviours in the company and regulate their direct reports and ensure controls are in place to regulate managers and supervisor's behaviours, as well as all staff.

In companies where the senior leaders either fail to or simply don't want to regulate behaviours of themselves and their senior staff, people with little emotional intelligence can climb ladders to senior positions. These people may struggle to manage let alone lead people and may even step on and disrespect others to further their career, boost their ego or achieve their goals. These people are not around every corner but can be present in less insightful companies. or parts of companies.

Among many inspirational and good leaders, I have also experienced the other end of the spectrum, and as the read progresses, I'll explain the impact that they and the companies who employed them had on my mental health and quite probably on the well-being of others.

I've come to learn over the years that we are all driven to do what we do by many factors, and looking back on leaders I've been at odds with, I should have focussed much more on the "why" they said and did what they did. In some cases, this may have helped lower conflict and stress, and in others, looking back, it would not have helped at all.

I'll also talk about what I've learned from being close to the inspirational and less inspirational leaders, both from whom I've drawn valuable lessons.

CHAPTER THREE

A Simplistic view of our brains

Mental illness

Our brains are amazing organs made up of multiple parts that do specific work for us, that are all linked through many pathways or routes. Apart from movement skills and enabling the five senses, different parts of the brain enable us to experience joy, happiness, sadness, love and a range of other emotions as well as feeling empathy for others and being able to retain and bring back long and short-term memories. Having read so much, many of the symptoms I have experienced during my life make a lot of sense.

Simply put, the longer chronic depression lasts and the more bouts that occur the more damage is done to the brain, and the longer recovery can take. The earlier treatment, be it talking, and recognition of the condition and/or medication starts the better chance there is for recovery.

Long term depression causes physical damage to the brain, which is shown as shrinkage of parts of the brain alongside the inability of the brain to develop new brain cells. This leads to interruption of pathways for signals to travel through the brain, meaning signals are not able to travel from one part of the brain to another, causing a variety of negative symptoms from memory loss to diseases such as Parkinson's disease.

My message in this section is that mental illness is an illness that is occurring because something has gone wrong in one or many of the parts of the brain or the pathways needed to send signals and it needs professional intervention.

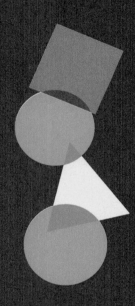

CHAPTER FOUR

My story

The beginnings of my story

From earlier life I suffered from anxiety at exam time with stomach pains. I was able to succeed and spoke about the stomach pains and was very lucky to have a Mum who had personal experience with mental illness.

I always looked up to everybody else, and from an early age lived with sense that I wasn't good enough at what I did, wasn't good looking and it goes on, despite there being no reason for me to feel this way in our household where we were all treated equally. This niggling, almost certainly DNA driven doubt about my own abilities stayed with me for many years, and even maybe until I fell off the "big cliff", and thankfully few such doubts exist today, I hope just sensible humbleness.

I was an asthmatic as a child, in and out of hospital by car

The beginnings of my story

and ambulance in a time when parents didn't stay overnight. Gasping for breath or not, come visiting times finishing, parents had to leave. School was an up and down time, with ten days in ten months of school owing to the asthma as a record. I don't remember the bad stories of children on the ward dying, that my mother can tell me and will never know if my early life had a bearing on my depression later in life.

At age eleven on the advice of doctors, I found running as a way out of the asthma. Running until I passed out, or least couldn't stand any more, my lungs slowly worked better. After this I was able to play sports with my brothers and friends. I played team sports up until I was no longer able to due to work and have stayed fit for most of my life and have found running an escape and coping mechanism over many years.

Able to run and walk, I became amazed by open country and especially mountains. I dragged my parents on walking holidays and went with friends camping to mountains. I had the young man's dream of living in a small cottage in mountains. My life took a different path, but I never lost my fascination with mountains.

Music and me

Music has had a profound impact on my life, in a way that I'm sure it has for many of you. I'm not a musician, don't read music but from an early age I was encouraged to listen to music. My mother and father loved classical music, as well as the popular singers of the time such as Dean Martin, Nat King Cole and others. From this early age, I enjoyed, indeed escaped the world through singing. However, my confidence was never high in my voice. I took part in a school shows but was labelled "baridrone" instead of baritone by a music teacher, who dented my confidence for many years.

Teachers are in so many ways leaders of the children they

teach and can have a profound impact on the children they teach positive and adversely.

Owing to my father's work, I became fascinated by rock opera, focussed on Andrew Lloyd Webber music (why is an entirely different story). I could sing every word of every musical of his and of other popular rock operas.

In addition to rock opera, there was still classical music as well as John Denver, Deep Purple, ELO and more.

Why have I told you about music and singing you may be starting to ask. Looking back on my life I have recognised that listening to music, singing and of course smiling is a thermometer of my state of mind. In my bad times, there has been a real lack of music listened to and sang. More on this later.

Live more in the day I moved to university and out to work. University was a means to an end – work and money. Potentially the start of the downfall, not focussing on the "now" and enjoying the University years. I was lucky in the sense that I come from a close family where we talk and gather as a family. My brothers have always been a massive part of my support network and I have spent many nights of fun with them, however on my way downhill, I failed to recognise the value of reaching out. At university, notably around exams, I recollect sitting in my room watching sad or happy events on TV with tears in my eyes. I considered myself silly, weak and too emotional. I never thought for a moment about mental illness and passed these moments and moved on, but they were etched on my mind.

At University running and music were coping mechanisms as well as occasional nights out with my brothers and numerous trips home, helped by the fact that I was only an hour away from home.

As university progressed and I went out to work, I lost touch with good friends, again a long-term pattern and a mistake. I argued to myself it was important to move forward, move on and this was to the exclusion of the past. To all my good friends of the past who may read this book, my sincere apologies for being a rotten friend.

Out to work, commuting to London each day from the same place, same time, same station with the same people (who made themselves busy with their newspapers). After a year I recognised this wasn't the world for me. An interview and two weeks later I was working in the energy industry in Northern Europe in a workshop and offshore. A new life and a new world, missing my family, but I was excited and clearly remember this.

I had been I the right place at the right time to have this new opportunity, and as the story unfolds it will clear that I have been fortunate to be in the right place at the right time several times throughout my career.

Manageable stress and friends

After a one-month trial, I entered one of the most stressful three months of my life, however, funnily, not the worst of my life, indeed an exhilarating time. Its correct, the right level of accepted stress is not a bad thing. Of thirteen starters we finished with seven, with people walking out and breaking down from anxiety and stress. I was learning something new every day and this has been a theme of my life and career, I recognise I need to keep learning and that I'm bored and tend to feel less motivated if I'm not learning for a long period of time.

Out of training school and off to Northern Europe for two years of intense work, long (twenty-four plus hours with no break), hard and cold days offshore, intense days preparing equipment and playing hard. This was a time of good memories, despite the constant hard days. There was anxiety and stress, but manageable and understandable given

'I lost contact with most of my friends from this good period and regret this.'

the weight on the shoulders of a (too young) team leader offshore. As was the industry, decades ago, it was only after eleven months that me and my line manager realised, I had worked these months without a day off. A long vacation was the solution to use up the days, which I thoroughly enjoyed.

However, working hard and making my way I had a constant feeling of not being good enough amongst the many other engineers. They were physicists, mathematicians and other impressive scientists. I had the capability and was doing fine, but had that small doubt alongside me, that followed me for many years. We had a wonderful social life and worked extremely hard and many hours. It was this social life, common stress and engagement with colleagues that kept us going. I've never been the best person at keeping in touch with friends and at this age and into my forties, didn't appreciate the amazing value and comfort of having people you call friends. I lost contact with most of my friends from this good period and regret this.

'We had a wonderful social life and worked extremely hard and many hours'

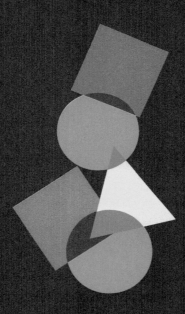

CHAPTER FIVE

Sing through it

Pushed beyond my limits

A new way of living

Yep, I met a girl (now my wife of three decades) which naturally led to change. The company I was with was a major international contractor who were happy to transfer me to South America to be closer to my, now fiancée.

A new location, new job, new everything and initially it was a good memory, learning a new language and culture and mixing with a like-minded fun team. In this role I experienced my first not so inspirational boss. The onshore manager of the offshore teams had power over the working crews. Short notice of jobs, brought about by apparent poor planning, led to horrendous hours of work, in many cases, seven days a week. I was young, enthusiastic and in love, but wasn't invincible.

Pushed beyond my limits

The long days, lack of appreciation and disrespectful approach of the manager got under my skin. In hindsight, I allowed him to get under my skin and I should have walked away from a job I wasn't enjoying and was driving me to mood swings. I was fortunate enough to have this capability, owing to the funds I had built up. But I was young, and wasn't this just how things really are?

Not only was I not enjoying the role, the conditions meant that I was pushing my teams harder than I was comfortable with, working twenty four hours and irregular hours, not seeing their families, which was simply contrary to my value set, one of which is caring for and respecting others. I'll come back to this term "value set" several times as this book progresses.

My values are a result of my DNA, upbringings and life experience. They are hard wired in my brain, are stronger than beliefs and much stronger than opinions.

This was my first experience of a company pushing me outside my values. It was surprising how hard this hit me and started me downwards to a condition where my emotions would go from desperately sad to angry in a second. This simply happened, I didn't ever think mental illness and in the oil and gas industry, this would have been a career killer in the 1980s. Living outside my value set has also been a common theme of downhill journeys, as opposed to working outside my comfort zone which has rarely stressed me, indeed it has usually invigorated me.

Stepping away for the first time

Eventually I did take the decision to walk out, resigning my role and speaking up to the regional head office about the treatment by the manager, only to learn that this was not the first occasion that he had caused a person to walk away. I was hired back into the company and moved to Scotland.

I'm
not
good
on my
own.'

My, now, fiancée was still in her home country and I was back to long, hard days on and offshore in the cold (but beautiful) North Sea. We were continents away and communicated through letters and photos and a phone call when we could afford it, an experience we cherish in the absence of today's social media capability.

Work was intense with little time to dwell on separation, except for days when there was a little calm, and on these days, I remember a sense of separation and sadness. For many years before and after I told myself I was fine being on my own, comfortable with my own company, and indeed for a while I can be. But I have come to realise in the last years that I do need company, and mostly that I need my family and friends and I'm not good on my own and as independent as I liked to make out. I suppose it was bravado and it was not sensible, as I've been through some of my very worst times on my own.

Landing on my feet

A year later, after the most incredible (it really was) wedding and honeymoon, it was back to Scotland as a married man. My wife and me spoke different languages still, and bumbled through conversations, but one thing was clear, twenty-five days a month offshore was not going to be sustainable for this marriage (or any for that matter). So, I quit my job, putting my family, my wife first. We moved to London to be with my parents and then to Middle England to do an M.Sc. We were happy, I passed the M.Sc. and walked into a role in South England. I had landed on my feet with a great company, team and job that pushed me in all the right ways. I visited countries in Europe, South Asia and South America alongside many parts of the UK. In this location, we bought our first house, with a bigger mortgage than we should have done.

I'm a dad and husband, and alike so many, financial stability and my ability to support my family has been an overriding factor in decisions I've taken in my career. I'll talk about this more as this book progresses.

After two cash strapped years an opportunity arose to move to South America where I was to set up a new division for the company I worked for in the UK. My wife was happy, at first. She was close to her family, in a Latin country and made friends quickly.

Hell bent on success

I moved to the new role with a bare bones business plan and goals to break even within the year. This was my first standalone shot as success, and I went for it. Seven days a week, twelve hours (plus) every day. I had a bed under my desk and clothes changes in the cupboard. Ridiculous I hear you say, and it was, but I was hell-bent on success for my wife and me and was proud. I should have shouted louder for help, demanded help, but I knew it wouldn't be appreciated and probably wouldn't come, so I battled on. I was project, legal, marketing and finance manager all in one and even took on the simultaneous translation at presentations. I trained and worked part time with my security team on Fridays and weekends to ensure I understood every aspect of the job, however, have to admit this was exhilarating.

I had let work take priority over family, something I should have learned from, but I didn't and in all honestly, I continued to fail in this respect until I "fell off the cliff" many years later, and this has left me with the biggest regrets of my life.

In a new job and new company in the same city, along came our wonderful and beautiful daughter. She was a handful of gargantuan proportions for us as new parents. We had wonderful times, but both spent too much time worrying about

Sing through it

Hell bent on success

her future, our future to the detriment of the present. I was the worst offender in this light and set about a trait that would be part of my later downfall. I became obsessed with providing for my family and saw the only way to do this was through hard work, success and more money. Maybe I should have asked them.

Failure to listen During this time, I regularly saw a doctor for stomach problems and was then diagnosed with high blood pressure. He was straight with me and advised that my work life balance was rubbish and I needed to find more down time. This advice was to be repeated to me many times with me listening and acting on the advice to varying degrees.

It was also in South America that I learned to scuba dive, an activity that would also become a wonderful escape from stressful workdays over many years. The underwater world is a calming and amazing world of wonder that over many years has been a calming influence on my life and going forward will be a much bigger part.

Money at any cost With my wife heavily pregnant with our twin boys when the company I worked for was merged with another and my job was cancelled. I had to provide in any way possible (or did I?) and took a job in North Africa whilst my wife went to the UK with my daughter to have my boys where, at the time, medical care was preferred.

An intense job, with long hours, tight deadlines and very difficult people in the team. I was in a role I enjoyed, but let the hours and load overtake me. We had a good social life, but nothing could prevent my first real brush with falling off the cliff. I was working hard, drinking hard and for a while even took up smoking. My moods were swinging wildly, and I would snap at colleagues the slightest provocation. Even a good social life, with weekends diving weren't enough to bring me back up enough to start the week, so I slowly went downhill.

A high point After my boys were born, as luck would have it, I was supposed to move with my family to a town in the North of the country, however the hospital wasn't set up for paediatrics and there were no jobs for me in in the capital city.

We moved to the UAE to a wonderful time in our lives. It was a safe and friendly place to bring up our children. My job covered much of the region and I was off on my travels again, and I thoroughly enjoyed the role, the challenges, the team and the travel. Over the range of countries there was work being done seven days a week and I was invariably on calls every day, including during vacation, however I

'I wrongly told myself the company needed me more than they really did.'

don't remember this overly stressing me, but yes annoyed me answering calls at 05:00 on vacation.

Taking my full vacation was also an issue. I invariably lost vacation days every year over many years as I wrongly told myself the company needed me more than they really did.

My country and the regional bosses were inspirational, and I was valued in my role. In one of my first senior leadership roles, the changes I was involved in were strongly supported by management regionally as well in the head office. As I would come to learn from Brett Read and Rod Ritchie of Safety Leaders many years later (in their leadership courses), we were

'I went for it. Seven days a week,
twelve hours (plus) a day.'

'My work life balance was rubbish,
I needed to find more down time.'

all aligned as to why the changes were needed, what benefits they would achieve, and I was left to determine the how.

My wife and me joked about my daughter asking, "are you going to Arn Daddy" (most places I visited ended with "an" such as Pakistan and Azerbaijan) before I left every time. Funny, yes, but it might have been a symptom of her ease with which I left the family house and my wife with three little children and the amount of time I was spending away. In the UAE I gained weight, and this was the second time told by a GP to slow down if I wanted to live to old bones.

Whereas it was a wonderful place to live, and we enjoyed many days, I was short tempered with my three little children too often, instead of enjoying their attention and accepting that being naughty was their way of testing boundaries and growing into a well-formed person, which I'm proud to say there are all now. Had I appreciated then that they are amazing at all ages, little and big, although trying at times.

We had a wonderful group of friends, who I am privileged to still call my friends after many years. In this role I was living in the day many days, maybe brought about by our young children. Good memories.

Making a good thing bad

Leaving the UAE and a wonderful team of people, we moved to the UK, to Scotland where we were immersed back in UK life. Four years passed, the children grew, and I progressed up the ladder in the company and was knocking at the door of a much more senior position. I was leading an amazing team of people and was involved in making fundamental changes to the way the business was run.

We were also cash strapped again with a decent mortgage and I became obsessed with the debt and providing

Good memories

A high point

a comfortable life for my family. For once I wasn't travelling much but made up for this with long hours at the office. I was becoming less patient, quicker tempered and withdrawn, as my children will attest to.

The reality was we were comfortable, in a comfortable house, in a wonderful suburb of a good town. I had a good job and had a wonderful boss and team, but I was ambitious and wanted more. We had a wonderful group of friends and enjoyed many days and nights. We even had a karaoke machine in the lounge, which we all had hours of fun with.

It was also during my time in Scotland that I was exposed to an inspirational coach called Ray Bell. Ray helped me and others understand the meaning of values as opposed to beliefs and opinions. He helped us map our careers, the ups and downs. The exercises demonstrated how we can take our worst career decisions and life decisions when we are gloomy and fed up. It showed that our best decisions were taken when we were flying high, positive and performing our best. I should have paid far more attention to lesson on values rather than career lessons. Never change on a downward cycle stuck with me and I certainly stayed in some roles afterwards for longer than I should trying to change the organisations I worked for, to become more aligned with my values whilst maintaining an eye on the bottom line. What I had to realise is that some battles can't be won and losing one battle doesn't mean you're on the down.

CHAPTER SIX

Climbing the career ladder

Eventually I got the call and an offer to climb into a higher position, in West Africa. It was not a dangerous place and our first experience of sub-Saharan Africa was an amazing and culturally enriching experience.

The office was a short drive from the compound we lived in, but down the only cross-town highway. This meant leaving the compound at 05:30 in the morning, long days and then anything up to three hours in a car travelling back to the compound at night weaving through the poorer areas or barrios of the city to make headway.

Adding to the stress of the role, a senior manager whom I reported to who was based in a UK office lacked an understanding of the realities on the ground and the difficulties of getting work done owing to a simple lack of exposure to the country, which may have had justifications I was not aware of. This lead to friction between me and the UK office on priority setting.

The reality was a bureaucratic national system, an emerging HSE culture of the workforce and a poor healthcare system. We had a small, but talented health team to care for thousands of employees and their families, both nationals and expats, in a country where haemorrhagic malaria and HIV were prevalent, amongst other health conditions and a staggering average age of death of 53, which was difficult to comprehend if you didn't live in the country.

'Best to hide my emotions for my daughter, wife and sons'

At the same time as this transition was occurring my oldest brother had been diagnosed with a rare form of cancer. Maybe for the first time I did put family first and made it clear I wouldn't move abroad whilst my brother was so ill. Without much more detail, my amazing brother has survived gruelling relapses in his cancer and continues as one of the most positive people I will ever know.

I will dwell on the role in West Africa, as looking back, I never rose out of this down period entirely.

Loading myself with stress

In the country I was based in and across other countries, we employed thousands of people who all had the potential to be hurt every day in the course of their work, as we all do every day, and I took everybody's well-being as my personal responsibility. Maybe admirable, but silly. I was there to advise

This
self-
doubt
was
illogical.'

and assist in setting strategies that would keep people safe and to ensure managers took accountability and responsibility for people's well-being. So, although I could blame hiccups during this period on others, I was also to blame in a large part for my own downhill journey in burdening myself with responsibility I didn't have to take. I was also dwelling far too much on what people thought about me, leaving meetings and engagements and playing it over in my mind a thousand times on my words and behaviours and if I could have done better. I had years in industry by now, had presented at conferences and universities as well at senior levels in companies, this self-doubt was illogical. I had the competence I needed to be in role but told myself otherwise.

A deep trough   Just over two years into the role, my daughter fell ill and barely made it out alive after being medically evacuated from country. Already heading downhill, this kicked me and my wife hard and pushed me to the edge of the cliff. In South Africa, sleeping next to my daughter (my wife was following on with the boys as there was not space in the evacuation plane) who was not guaranteed to make it, I couldn't sleep, was crying (not my normal behaviour) on every call with family whilst trying to keep the job going with the help of an amazing Health and Safety Manager in country and a senior colleague in London, all the time under fire from my line manager who said the right words, then complained about me not answering emails on time.

I did my best to hide emotions for my daughter, wife and sons and simply didn't talk about the desire just to curl up in a dark corner and go to sleep. My mother was a wonderful support in this time, being remote and understanding the entire set of symptoms. My mother was the limit of who I could break down with. I had to be strong for my family, provide for them and had to be strong in the office on my return. This was the oil and gas industry; indeed, this was industry, and despite the employee assistance programs and talk of well-being that were indeed well meant, mental illness was not a conversation I would have wanted to have if I wanted my job.

If only I had known what was coming and how far down, I was to go, I'd have shouted it out loud, and trusted the systems.

By the end of this year, disillusioned and tired of many of the characteristics of the company and senior management, I moved onto another role.

It was during this time in West Africa that I started drinking very heavily, mostly at weekends. Drinking was a way out for many in the stressful environment we worked in and yes, many people drank to excess (got drunk) but I took that to the extreme. I knew it was wrong, but it was an escape for the muddle and mess in my mind. Alcohol slowed the muddle down for a short while, until I went past a sensible number. I became grumpy with my wife and children and knew many days when I woke up with a hangover how wrong it was, the drinking and the way I treated my family. Again, my family were taking the brunt of my depression.

The self-doubt was still omnipresent. With too much drink in us all, many of us spent memorable (yes, I do remember) nights singing and simply being guys. One night a good friend and work colleague invited to sing with him at his birthday bash. He had an amazing band and invited me to sing Hotel California, by the Eagles. Despite the wonderful atmosphere, the ease of this song, and having the words in front of me, I sang a crazy abstract version and walked away embarrassed to our table to drink. He gave me a wonderful opportunity to step out of my shell, and I tanked. This stayed with me for many years, the kindness of the opportunity and my inability to simply enjoy the moment.

I touched on the "making change" in the role in Scotland, and this is a state where I am happiest. In a large company I was less able to influence decisions and was "told" what to do more than I was comfortable with and had been looking for a role where I had greater freedom to influence company decisions and found it.

After West Africa, we discussed returning to the UK, but the location of the new position was attractive, as was the salary. I'm not certain that if we had returned, I wouldn't have ended up not falling off the cliff. I doubt it as I was still making the same mistakes and not learning.

The continued road downwards

The continued road downwards

The new job was back in the UAE, a country we were already comfortable in. We had a ready-made group of amazing friends we had known before and were happy and enjoying the social. These were people I could have spoken to and tried to speak to but was embarrassed to talk about the reality of my mental state.

Expatriate life has its perks, but also its downsides. Employers don't expect expats to need to learn and pay for a pound of flesh (competence and the willingness to work hard, excessively often). As exciting as the new job was, it brought with it the stress of introducing change to a company, where some people are simply more comfortable than others. I had the bulk of the senior leadership and managers on board with the changes that I had agreed to bring in, however struggled with some senior team members. I should have taken more time to get alignment on why changes were required and the benefits before launching into action, as this struggle and the friction it brought were significant stressors.

Vacation is also an opportunity to switch off from work and enjoy a different time. I, as so many colleagues, worked up to last minute to enable me to answer as few emails as possible on vacation. Yes, I know there should be none, but that was rarely the case. Being under increasing pressure up to the last minute, so often resulted in falling ill in early in the vacation ruining the down time for me and family. This was almost certainly the result of the adrenalin that was continuously being produced as a result of the stress, suppressing my immune system.

It was the travel that told most on me and my family rather than the opposition to change. I was travelling every month to businesses that were struggling, and once again I took it on myself to drive the change towards improved business success and for the protection of the people who worked for the company and to improve the performance of the company.

On the theme of values, an influential company on the company I worked for regularly promoted decisions that were often not aligned with my values, and once it again it told on me, as I tried to swim against the prevailing current.

The company and the job had become my life again, my work life balance completely unbalanced in the wrong direction. I should note that the CEO and management team, with whom I worked, were admirable, respectful and good people and we were really like a family at work under exceptional stresses.

There were exciting times, and times of stress. Instability was also a theme in this new role. The threat of the role coming to an end owing to the company situation was always there, and this played on my mind, as a major threat to my ability to provide for my family.

I was still a grumpy, and at times an angry dad, not a very loving husband and was drinking too much. I would drink wine and then move to whiskey, which I've always liked, but now it became part of a bad schedule. Years later one of my boys recounted the story of me going to my boys' room, drunk and telling my boys they would amount to nothing. I'm dreadfully ashamed of this type of behaviour and the impact it has potentially had on my boys and my daughter. I didn't miss work during this time owing to my drinking and depression but was certainly less effective some days.

I don't want to belittle nor forget the good times we had over many of our years in the UAE, wonderful gatherings with friends and family. My parents were regularly visitors, and there were many nights sitting around the kitchen table joking with our children and even their friends, our house, for some reason being the gathering place for their friends. We had gathered a family of stray cats in the yard and then another stray cat, who gave us days of joy and grief when some passed away.

'I don't want to belittle nor forget the good times'

'My parents were regularly visitors, and there were many nights sitting around the kitchen table joking with our children and even their friends, our house, for some reason being the gathering place for their friends.'

'I don't want to belittle nor forget the good times'

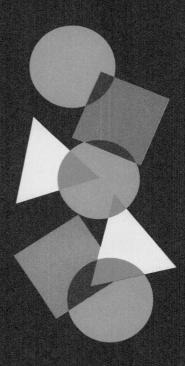

CHAPTER SEVEN

No stopping the fall

Coping mechanisms such as running, the gym and scuba diving were not enough to keep me on track in life. I remember one weekend vividly as an example of my mood. As a family we visited the UAE East coast. My daughter and one son had learned to dive a year or so before. We were kitting up in wet suits and I can remember my son struggling with his wet suit. Instead of stopping my preparation and sitting with him to help him, I was grumpy and impatient. He didn't enjoy the weekend much, I wonder why?

I was in and out of doctors and gastroenterologists with stomach problems and headaches. The doctors found nothing wrong, except for a common piece of advice "slow down your doing damage to yourself, its stress related".

After five years I bid a sad farewell to this company and left a little bit of me there, and in hindsight, should have stayed. But I was chasing a bigger role and landed a role in an international company with a larger operational presence in the region. I was pleased with the legacy I had left, but thought I needed more, needed bigger. The money was like the last role; however, I saw this as another step on my career path. There were similar challenges to the previous role, and travel to multiple countries that took me away from the family.

It was about this time that my daughter started to go downhill with increasingly extreme anxiety that impacted her life and all our lives profoundly. Not only were my boys and wife having to put up with me, but now had to contend with an out-of-control sister whose behaviours were probably not atypical from other adolescents struggling with extreme anxiety.

It was also a time of change. After nearly three years of excitement in my new job, where the management team were working in concert to drive positive change, the job changed dramatically, once again with many decisions that ran contrary to my values and were out of my control.

Choosing your battles

Once again, I was battling a tidal wave of decisions that troubled me owing to the potential impacts they could have, and I should have easily seen I was going to get washed away, at least washed along and damaged. I was clearly knocking and sometimes kicking on firmly closed and solid doors and didn't pick my battles carefully.

Many changes, although, were successful and were consensus decisions of most of the leadership, so not every day was a bad day.

At this same time, I perceived I was pulling away from my wife, my family and friends. Had I known the impacts of the chemicals released during depression attacking and damaging the brain I might have understood this pulling away. Years and years of damage from excess stress brought on partly by jobs and circumstances as well as self-doubt had bombarded my brain and done its damage.

As part of my recovery, I have read much about the chemistry of stress and the impacts on the brain and body, and I remain worried for the longer term impacts it may have had. Time will tell, but for now, I'm positive.

Increasing symptoms denied

Signs of anxiety had crept up on me. Personal and small administrative tasks were sparking fear. I was constantly late on expenses (months). I would gather the receipts, pull up the form on my computer and then freeze, putting them off to yet another day. Simple administrative phone calls for personal reasons were becoming anxiety triggers and I started to avoid them, with my wife picking up much of the load.

My daughter was getting treatment and thankfully improving, but I was still slipping downhill. I was working long hours, weekends, travelling every month and becoming more withdrawn. Decisions were being taken at work impacting my team, which were not debates, but ultimatums. The red lights were flashing everywhere warning me to move on and move out of the way, but I wasn't moving.

I was outwardly bright at work, but at home grumpy and drinking too much, wine, whiskey, vodka and more, basically whatever we had in the house. 'Bright at work and socially' was a theme of every situation I found myself in over the years. Putting on bright face for those outside the house was what I did, but stupidly I wasn't that bright at home and my family suffered from my moods over many years. Listening to professionals and colleagues who have opened up, this is a common pattern. Indeed, being overly bright was a symptom of mine and I've seen this in others I've worried about.

'Time will tell, but for now,

I'm positive'

More threads added My parents visited us many times and on a visit about five years into our UAE life, it was clear my Father was not himself; he was withdrawn and quiet. Sometime after returning home my father was diagnosed with Alzheimer's. My father was a proud man and the certainty of losing control over his own life and body and the known future of symptoms was not something he was going to take easily, as I'm sure nobody ever will, whilst there is no effective treatment. He tried to commit suicide more than once, having a profound impact on the entire family and especially my mother. My middle brother, who lived closest to my parents took the brunt of these events having to call ambulances and cleaning up the mess. I can't imagine the impact on him. I started travelling back to UK more, whenever I could, putting family higher up the agenda, maximising all my days off to spend time back in the UK.

Whereas coming back to the UK to visit family was something I looked forward to and will never regret, it meant there was no real annual getaway from everything. That might sound strange and heartless, however removing yourself from your life every now and then is important. I would call it a mental detox.

This is a long-term theme, not just mine, but of many people who have had to follow work abroad. Vacations are an opportunity to go home to visit family. Whereas this is a wonderful time and needed to reconnect, and for children to connect, it means that there is no absolute 'getaway' holiday to totally de-stress. This lack of getaway time can build over the years, coupled with a high stress job and have an incremental impact.

My father was moved to a psychiatric unit where he would be safer. My mother fell off the cliff with another mental break down driven by my father's suicide attempts and deteriorating mental capability. My oldest brother was ill and my middle brother taking a well-earned break, so I travelled back to England to care for my mother. This was a hard experience, seeing my mother emaciated, however I had a job to do, and my state of mind was not as important as my Mother's well-being. I worked through the confusing world of government supplied psychiatry to eventually get my mother into a psychiatric unit as near to home as possible. It was far from ideal, but my father was in the unit closest to home. Eventually my father and mother were to end up in the same care home where they had dementia care capabilities thanks to the efforts of my middle brother. Seeing my Father's dementia progress turned my mind to growing older, and the clear fact that most of my life was behind me. Amongst the many other layers of worry and anxiety, I had built another in the fear of getting older, how much time I had left and how could I make the most of those years. I saw a life of work in front of me, which I wasn't enjoying, and no manner in which I might enjoy the future. In summary, the failing light at the end of the tunnel had disappeared.

In talking about managing my mother into care, I talk about crises bringing out the calm me, the clear thinking me, be they in business or family. I've saved my daughter's life from a difficult choking event, worked with my mother on her care, attended a vehicle accident caring for a victim until the ambulance arrived and have responded to a number of industrial emergencies at local, regional and corporate level including fatalities and on one tragic occasion the death of the child of a colleague. Even in my lowest state I was able to turn into a different person in a crisis or emergency. This not to say, that after the event, the emotional impact hasn't been there, indeed some events will never be truly out of my system and can choke me up to think about them after many years.

After speaking to professionals, I've come to understand this as the capability to compartmentalise in the brain, where you can push everything aside to deal with the moment. And indeed, from my darkest moments I remember blurred times where my brain has done a good job at eliminating certain memories or at

'Crisis bringing out the calm in me, the clear thinking me'

least in "fuzzing" them. Maybe not science but my experience.

We moved to a smaller house in the UAE to save money and then onto an apartment to save more money as our children went to universities. It was the right financial decision but the wrong life decision. We were comfortable in the house we had been in for nearly five years, with a garden and the cats and weren't comfortable again in the UAE.

Knowing my mental state was deteriorating, and knowing that self-doubt was there, I embarked on a course to become a Dive Master. This is a scuba diving qualification that permits you to assist starter divers under water. I knew I had the capability, experience and calm demeanour under water. But my lack of self confidence told the inner me, that I was going to fail. I had passed the exam, which wasn't easy, completed the bulk of the course, then started travelling again for work. Instead of overcoming the doubt, and returning to complete the course, I consciously focussed on work, until the time to course had expired and made this my excuse for not passing. I'm still diving, but sincerely regret letting this opportunity go.

Empty Nest

My children started leaving home for university and my wife and me were alone together. We had spoken of this time for so many years, how we would go out to dinner, nights out and we wouldn't have to worry about the children out at night. But it was the opposite, we worried about the children so many miles away and how quickly we could get there if they needed us. I couldn't be the caring person I should have been for my wife who missed the children who she had cared for everyday and every year for all their lives. My wife has been the most incredible supportive and loving wife and mother I could ever have wished for, and I now understand and regret my struggles have had a profound impact on her life and happiness.

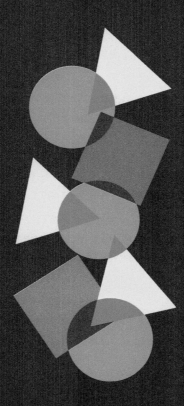

CHAPTER EIGHT

Blurred memories

Looking back on the year or months I'm moving to, it is a blur, fuzzy in my head on timings of events. This is common for stressful periods of my life, they are unclear, messy memories and sometimes absent, as opposed to happier times that are clearer in my head.

And so, the downhill journey continued. I was becoming more withdrawn, snappier, and sometimes too bright at the office, taking days off when I just couldn't get out of bed. There were simply days when my body couldn't function. Other days I went to the office and had to come home and go to bed. I was skipping gatherings with our friends of many years, my brain went into hyperdrive and shut down mode thinking of going out. Simple administrative tasks like making a phone call to the bank or filling out a form became unimaginably stressful.

If I pushed myself, I could feel the anxiety rising in my whole body and especially my head where the "fuzz" would spread and again I moved towards shut down mode and sleep. Fuzz is certainly not a scientific term; however, it best describes the feeling I was experiencing every day. I've also heard people refer to it a fog.

I couldn't stand looking in the mirror at myself. I was old and ugly and simply unhappy being me.

I touched on a thermometer of my mental state earlier, and looking back I never sang during this time, it just wasn't on the menu of things I did. I remember trying to lift my mood by trying to sing, watch bright TV programs, watch sport, run, but it wasn't working, and I couldn't bring myself to sing nor listen to music. Smiles were reserved for when I was drinking, or they were required at work.

I was travelling frequently again and dreading every trip, knowing my efforts would make little difference to the direction of the company and anything I did try to achieve would be met with scepticism at the best as a I swam against the strong tide. I need to add that the people I worked with were good, intelligent and respectful people.

I had started to fall back into the trap of taking on too much responsibility for the hours in a day and treating the job as my life to the detriment of my home life. A respected leadership consultant told me, one evening, in very clear terms how stupid he saw me behaving, taking the world on my shoulders. I did listen to him, took on the lesson, but unfortunately, I was already halfway down the hill and slipping fast.

Falling off a cliff

My wife had to travel to the UK for an extended period to be with the children for multiple good reasons, which we had discussed and agreed on.

In my already depressed state, the loneliness, that I had never acknowledged before, was the end of the road for me. We agreed she had to go for our children and that it was the best for the family, but I hadn't realised that despite our not getting on well, she was the rock I was able to hold onto to stop me going under water. Sorry for the clichéd "rock" reference, but is the right word, a solid and unmoving part of my life.

Chronic or deep depression is so often the result of more than one factor or cause. For me, the multiple converging threads came together, and I crashed or burned out a month or so after my wife travelled to the UK.

The following section is my best recollection of the period of time. Events don't sit clearly in my mind and times are muddled and some time frames missing altogether. How I felt and thought are bad memories, that has left me with a deep desire never to go to that place mentally again and an even deeper desire to help others to prevent or stop the slide towards this place or worse.

I couldn't go to work, wasn't sleeping for nights on end, was drinking heavily and was extremely unstable at work. My performance had gone downhill and I wasn't able to focus on anything for more than a few minutes. My head felt like there was an action movie of my life playing at 1000 mph all day every day and even when I could find short periods of time of less anxiety, I experienced the head fuzz, a feeling where there was a fog impacting every thought, every decision. I would snap and was 'far too honest' with my views at work, to the extent that it was not professional.

What was my rock bottom?

I was sleeping at irregular times in the day, walking for hours around the area of the office, as I didn't feel capable of going into the office. Just stepping out of the lift was terrifying.

At night I would walk for hours in the sweltering summer heat trying to avoid crowds, indeed trying to avoid people.

Sing through it

Blurred Memories

Eating was a chore, and I was losing weight quickly, adding to the tiredness.

I was speaking to my wife and children most nights and did my very best to appear normal, which I did well as looking back with my wife, she had no indication I was spiralling downwards.

I was no longer capable of being bright for others and it became clear to the office that I was not the person I had been. My emotions were a violent series of highs and lows, troughs followed by trough then a wave of feeling OK, then back into another trough. I was now falling off the cliff and there was no clear way in my head to stop me falling and I had ceased trying to halt the fall, there was no energy left in me.

A TV program, news article or thought could result in me sobbing uncontrollably. I was drinking to excess every night. Suicide was truly an option considered multiple times if not all the time, sitting on the floor of the apartment for hours on end. Living on the 24th floor of a building it was a simply a step off. I saw that I was no longer capable of providing for my family and shouldn't be liked by family after the years of bad behaviour, anger, drinking and absence. I could see that their futures would be better served by my not being alive.

'In a world I can now best describe as dark and darker clouds gathering around me'

I was getting older and what did it matter if I died now or later. The thoughts came and went in a world that I can now best describe as dark and darker clouds gathering around me.

There was also a feeling of detachment from who I was, detachment from my wife notably, which looking back was simply illogical, however now entirely logical given my understanding of the impacts of depression on the brain and the area of the brain that deals with the higher senses such as love.

It was the thought of the impact on my family that pulled me back every time from the brink. I'm thankful I never went that one step further as I still held onto the knowledge that there would be immediate grief for all my family.

I perceived I had nobody to reach out to in this state. I was ashamed of my state, my behaviours and my increasing inability to work and my perceived failure. I should have been confident talking to my wife, brothers and friends, but so deep was the shame and desperation, that I didn't know what I would say. It was easier to say nothing.

I had spoken to our Human Resource Manager on some symptoms and difficulty at work. He, along with his team were an immense support going forward, but it was a lighter conversation than it should have been as I wasn't comfortable opening up.

Sing through it

'

What was my rock bottom?

lighter

'It was a conversation than it should have been'

CHAPTER NINE

A defining moment

I had struggled to get up and go into the office one morning. I was tired, angry and devoid of focus. The fog in my head was thick and the pressure in my head indescribable.

Sitting at the desk, with a coffee on the desk untouched, I couldn't focus on the computer screen. When my eyes did decide to focus, I tried to work on a spreadsheet with no success, I didn't remember how to work a spreadsheet, the commands had gone from my head. I couldn't face another meeting that meant nothing to me. People talking to me were noise, I couldn't focus on what they said, it was garbled, and my emotions were up and down in violent cycles. I should have been attending a management meeting, and watched the attendees going past me and it meant nothing. I was totally detached from me. It felt like I had moved on and this uncontrollable being was in my place. I'd like to describe that morning in more detail, but I simply don't remember much.

The piece of me that was still present had two options. One was to go back home, and I'm not sure how that option would have ended up, and the other to find some form of help out of this mess in my head.

At around 10:00 am. I walked out of the office in a daze, holding back tears and somehow walked (I have no recollection of this walk, nor anything else much of that day) to a trusted clinic and asked to see a GP. I couldn't hold it together, had tears in my eyes and had trouble simply moving as my legs felt like lead weights.

This is an example in this story where I am still thankful that I had access to this help thanks to a company health insurance. I waited and was given an appointment with a doctor who was wonderful, listened and immediately prescribed a set of drugs to help me sleep as well as calm me down, with a massive warning "don't drink". I was now going cold turkey on alcohol, and yes, I was dependent on the momentary escapes from alcohol, or so I thought, at the same time as trying to come to terms with what had happened. I was in total denial concerning mental illness. My mother, my father and others, but surely not me.

I knew how I felt but couldn't comprehend the future with this stigma. Talking about the condition was hard at first and yes, I was ashamed of the perceived weakness, a condition I knew would be frowned on by some in my company, by industry and generally by society. After so many years of mental illness being highlighted and talked about this should not have been the case, but it was and is still reality in many companies and in society and needs to stop.

That same day or the next (blurred memory) I saw an experienced psychologist who was a practiced listener. It was good but uncomfortable to talk and break down crying more than I've cried since in the hospital with my daughter in South

Africa. I continued to see the psychologist who helped and had great value. Talking through my fears and the threads that has brought me to this place was good. She took me back many years and helped me piece together many of the events and experiences from the past that may not have been recognised as triggers or symptoms of depression. She also helped me understand how to talk about my current state of mind and the reason behind many of the symptoms such as total emotional detachment, inability to focus and the feeling of being worthless.

It is thanks to this psychologist that I have been able to piece together this book after a long time gathering the pieces and threads of my life.

After a period of weeks of severe ups and downs in mood and mental state I was advised to see a respected and to the point psychiatrist. After a series of questions into my current state and past, he, in a matter-of-fact way described to me what had happened in as technical terms as I might understand and proceeded to prescribe a different treatment regime. Amongst other pieces of invaluable advice, he told me that sleep had to be at the top of the priority list, as well as zero alcohol for the foreseeable future.

This advice and treatment change are a time I recognise as the real start of the upward climb and my journey to where I am today. I was off the booze, sleeping with the help of medication and slowly accepting the situation for what it was. I was suffering from depression and almost certainly had done so for years, although I acknowledged depression in my head, saying it out loud was more difficult.

I had been told and recognised that the treatment or drugs I was taken would take a number of weeks to start to work. In this interim period, I remember days where I slept a lot and others where I was able to cope better.

'I was a little like a **robot**, not able to show much emotion'

Climbing back up to a brighter place

My company human resources team were understanding and gave me the time off that was prescribed. Pay quickly went down to a fraction of my usual salary, that should have worried me, but I was unable to worry about this in my state. I knew that what I was doing was now critical. My psychiatrist was clear that if I went back too early or went down the same avenue again, I would not be able to work again. This was now advice that I had to listen to.

After a short trip to the UK, where I was detached and not the person I should have been for my daughter's graduation and boys' birthday, I returned to the UAE, closely followed by my wife.

I had ceased to be a very close and caring person and remember a less happy time together, entirely down to my behaviours. As my psychologist explained to me the part of the brain that controls emotions such as "love" was damaged and I was a little like a robot, unable to show much emotion.

My wife and me found that talking about my condition openly was difficult, as my wife, understandably, could still only see the uncaring me and still wasn't certain if the depression had caused them or was an excuse for the behaviours. Because of my lack of emotion, I was not an easy person to live with and couldn't flick a switch to be caring and happy.

I've spoken to family members with depression and seen that life is often just as hard for the partner dealing with the depression, mood swings and other varied symptoms. My wife, me and so many others had also grown up in a world where depression was not recognised, and it was given other names. It may have been a passing subject if we heard of a person committing suicide, but even then, it wasn't a subject, at least in our families, we would dwell on.

I was still not comfortable talking about my condition. I was ashamed, but increasingly less so. I started to talk about

Sing through it

Jumping the gun

symptoms, notably the consistent fight or flight reaction from my brain that wanted to fly, which resulted in the need to sleep far more than normal.

My wife and me started to talk about symptoms however not so much about words such depression and anxiety. This would take time. Hiccup days were still times of tension as I was withdrawn during these periods at home and not the easiest of people to be with.

Jumping the gun   I tried to get back to work a little early, but it was a clear failure and within two days was back at home. Arriving at the office at my normal 07:30 I sat at my desk, tried to be sociable, tried to be bright, tried to log-on to my computer. Nothing was working. My body and head wanted to shut down within minutes. The flight in fight or flight was winning over. The warning the psychiatrist had given me rung loud in my head, and I calmly explained to the HR team that I had jumped the gun and walked slowly back to metro station and home. At home, I could nothing but sleep, I was physically drained for days after this.

On good advice I was "listening to my body" sleeping when I needed to and exercising like crazy when I could. Exercise became a distraction rather than an escape and even better it was something my wife and me could do together. Doing things together was something we hadn't done for a long time, except visiting friends. Exercise also released the right chemicals in my body driving a more positive attitude. I was however careful, as exercise drives temporary mood changes, that you can come off quickly.

As I slowly started to reintegrate with friends, attending gatherings mostly with close friends only. I had decided to be open about my quiet or absent times and spoke as freely as I was comfortable to about what had happened. It was fascinating how different people engaged, didn't engage or just looked awkward when talking about what had happened, notably the word depression.

I did return to work for a short period of time to help out on an emerging project with the understanding I was recovering and thank the local management of that company for allowing me to go back knowing I still wasn't at my best. In my recovering state it was good to get back to thinking and engaging with people and making a difference. During this short time, I drank many coffees with colleagues and was frightened by how many were able to recognise my symptoms in themselves at that time or in the past and were surprised with my open admission of suffering from depression and the burnout.

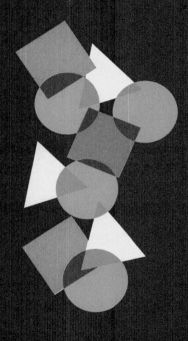

CHAPTER TEN

Back on track

My recovery continued slowly, and I became more aware of my mistakes of the past. I didn't dwell on them but focussed on them to learn from. I was climbing from where I had been and it felt better, not great, with the occasional step backwards that could last hours, a day or more. My entire outlook on life was changing. I was becoming confident in my own abilities and far less worried about what people thought of me. I continued to exercise for me to feel good and for my health, and not beat times and distances as I had before, piling more pressure on myself.

I had left my previous company and was out of work and not worried. I was focussing on my recovery. I knew I would get back into work, and that my newfound relaxed manner was a benefit to everybody around me. My children were clear with me in the difference they saw, they liked it and we were having more fun. This lack of fun at home and my grumpy moods and snappy temperament with my children and wife is a guilt I will feel for all my days, however its past and I can only change the future.

I was getting back to diving when I could, and at times simply being close to the sea. It is true that the sea, calm or rough, is an amazingly beautiful aspect of this earth. I can be next to and the in the sea as much time as possible.

I was becoming easier with doing nothing or more accurately sitting quietly and observing. Observing the view, the people going past, the trees, plants and taking in the detail. This might sound clichéd and romantic, but it is something I now enjoy and have not done for many years, if ever.

Acceptance of who and how I am

With professional and self-help, I've come a long way up the road of recovery. It's a bumpy road with the occasional pot hole. I refer to the place I've come from as "falling off the cliff" as this is the analogy that best makes sense for me. I was sliding down a hill for many years, the slope got steeper, until I was at the edge of the cliff. I fell off, but thankfully have been able to climb back up a little battered and bruised. I'm not ashamed or worried about using the terms such as depression and anxiety, but I'm not a professional and prefer to use many of the terms I've used in this book.

I can now accept hiccups for what they are, and I don't feel guilty about them, however they are disappointing and occasionally worrying, a reminder of worse times. Hiccups, or not so good days, are characterised by difficulty sleeping and a fuzzy head, but they are getting further apart, and I'm learning to deal with them and most importantly to speak to my family about these days, so they know how I'm feeling and understand why I might be quieter, need time alone listening to music or why I go to bed early.

Hiccup days no longer mean I can't function, I can and do and am effective. I may work a slightly shorter day at these times, but get the job done, as today I enjoy my job and relish most of the challenges thrown my way.

I'm in a senior role that has its pressures, but I manage them. I work for a company that, and I say this truthfully, that has a healthy balance between performance and well-being and that cares. In short, I work for a company that has values aligned to my own, contrary to many positions I have stayed in for too long in the past.

I take time to plan the week and months ahead striving to ensure that my team and me can achieve our goals without adverse impacts on our well-being.

I'm still on low doses of medication I was started on after the burnout and if I don't take them, I do feel the effects, much like a hiccup day. The doses are half the original dose and I'm hoping to eliminate these altogether eventually, but that's for the future.

I've found doctors to be listeners on mental health who encourage me to tell them what I'm capable of in reducing medication and when. Good advice, such as not reducing medication in winter, when days are shorter has been listened to.

Occasional experiments such as raising the dose for a few days to counter a down period, have been ill advised and contrary to good practice, and have had unexpected impacts on my mood, making me erratic and almost delirious, so no more of that.

It's OK to be emotional on occasions now. An emotional TV program or YouTube video can make me well up with tears as can an emotional song listened to or sang and that's OK, that's me, although I'm still not entirely comfortable showing this much emotion when not on my own.

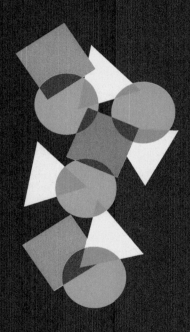

CHAPTER ELEVEN

Ending up

And now to end this book. I've learned so much about myself, my past, my genetic makeup, how I work and the impact that my long fight with anxiety and depression has had on those I love, and how wonderful life really is and should have been for most of my life.

I have realised how the cumulative damage I have inflicted in myself and was inflicted by life's ups and downs, led to where I ended up. I have learned to listen to my body and mind as well as those around me. I'm careful with stress now, managing workload, family and me time purposefully. I advise to the best of my ability with my now thirty-six years-experience and am still passionate about making a positive difference to people's lives and the impact the company I work for can have on people's lives and the planet balanced with commercial and energy realities.

Ending up

Again, I look back on my life of experiences, travel, people I've met and the changes I am confident I've made in people's lives over the years and I would change much in how I have handled those experiences but not the experiences themselves.

I stated earlier, that I still have "hiccup days" and indeed a few days sometimes when I feel less enthusiastic about life, but then so does everybody. I recognise these days as part of the recovery and respect them. Recovery is a word that I need to understand better, as a full recovery might mean going back to where I was before, but for me it's about going so far past where I was. It's recovering the person I always should have been.

Sundown can be a hard time of the day and I still occasionally feel that a drink might brighten up my day but know the truth in that alcohol is a depressant that won't really help. I do have a drink at weekends, sticking to

'It's is recovering the person I always should have been.'

beer or wine with no spirits allowed. I talk about this to my family openly and am clear that I do still enjoy a few glasses of red wine and as long as I can remain in charge.

I've recently found that alcohol can have some unwanted interactions with one drug I'm taking that means, in simple terms, I'm less able to control my drinking and can see large mood shifts in a short time. Until I experienced these mood swings, I was too relaxed on medications and alcohol, and notably anti-depressant and mood stabilisers, no more. They can and often do react and if zero alcohol is best, then that's the case, it's not a big deal after a short while. This especially true when you read the frightening impacts of continued excessive alcohol intake on the brain. Alcohol is, and should be, thought of as a recreational drug as it is taken for enjoyment, socialising and can have harmful effects on your whole body.

Breaking news as I write version forty one of this book, I'm off alcohol completely after a nasty experience where I felt like I was slipping downwards fast again. Insomnia has kicked back in and I had a night where I had no option but to walk in the early hours of the morning to stop my head exploding. The images at 1000mph were there again. It will be a struggle, but it's just not worth it anymore. This will be a struggle, and more of this in a later edition.

I'm sensibly nervous about the future, I'm OK with mortality and whereas I don't want to die, accept that we all have to take that road. I am looking towards a bright future whatever it consists of. I'm getting older and I can't run the times I used to, but so what, I can still run, dive, swim and be a fool with my very big kids and of course sing. I'm eager for real adventure, I have a bucket list of things I want to achieve and do and am planning these, not just talking. Some are may seem crazy, like diving in a tiger shark's (and more sharks) natural environment and more on my list.

I'm singing at times when I feel like I can and have started to record a few songs, that aren't of great quality, but I'm slowly getting comfortable listening to my own voice after many years of cringing. I'm getting better at looking at the mirror and accepting me in my skin and look forward to the day when I am truly happy being me.

My daughter, who suffered from anxiety for years, now has a Master's degree and is happy and I'm so proud, as I am of my boys.

My father died last November after years with dementia. Seeing him slip downwards was hard, as it is for anybody who goes through this, and the last few days were heart breaking. Thankfully he was surrounded by family, care home staff that loved him and had the support of a local hospice to ensure he was comfortable. I will always miss him in my life.

I've seen mental illness is still not as well as accepted in society as we would like to make out. Some people still see it as a taboo subject and a weakness, somebody who is unreliable and should be passed over, so heavens help me in my mid 50's with mental illness.

It does take courage to reach out sometimes. We need to recognise that anxiety, depression and other forms of mental illness is not failure, weakness or your fault and that it is an illness just like any other illness and there are millions of people like you and me and that they are probably close to you. Just like any illness, we need to reach out, talk and ask for help. Many companies do have effective employee assistance programs and there are help lines you can call, all of which you should use.

This book was easy and not easy to write. It brought back troubling memories for me and others, however it has helped me piece together the jigsaw of life experience, successes and failures, but most of all how I failed to listen to profession advice, my family, my body and my mind. I also failed to react or remove myself from roles where my capability to impact positive change had ended and/or the company was moving in a direction against my fundamental values. Talking to or telling somebody how I felt, the reasons for my mood swings and or getting help much earlier in life, recognising the symptoms of depression may well have averted my eventual downfall.

The Last Page

If this book and what is contains in it helps just one person recognise themselves in my description of the past and they can stop the decline and move upwards and reach out and talk about how they feel it has been worth the time to write. Please reach out and talk if you feel down, anxious, unable to cope at any time, for any length of time. Your family, friends, work colleagues and so many see this state as simply a result of many factors and NOT weakness indeed to talk and speak IS strength.

Mental illness is caused by real changes happening in your brain brought about by external events, conditions or something going wrong inside you, it is an illness that needs medical attention.

Being the occasionally pedantic me, I was going to make a list of key learnings from this book, but maybe its best you take your own key messages away.

Be happy folks and please look out for yourselves and others who may be suffering or on the start of the downward hill towards the cliff. Let's, make sure we walk, and we walk them back up the hill to the place I'm in today.

Thank you so much for reading this far, I truly appreciate your time.

John

Printed in Great Britain
by Amazon

69539745R00059